Laura Heisler and Sasha Eden in a scene from the New York production of *BFF*.

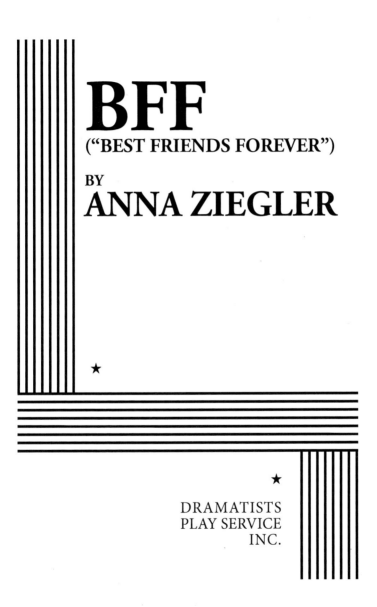

# BFF
## ("BEST FRIENDS FOREVER")

BY
## ANNA ZIEGLER

★

★

DRAMATISTS
PLAY SERVICE
INC.

BFF ("BEST FRIENDS FOREVER")
Copyright © 2008, Anna Ziegler

All Rights Reserved

## NOTE ON BILLING

## SPECIAL NOTE ON SONGS/RECORDINGS

*This play is dedicated to my family*
*(which includes David, to whom, of course,*
*all things are dedicated).*
*With all my love.*

# ACKNOWLEDGMENTS

Thanks to Maureen Towey, Sarah Benson, Jason Grote and the Soho Rep Theatre Lab from 2004–2005, the group who nurtured this play from its inception. Thanks also to Kim Rosenstock and Ars Nova, to the Lark's Arthur Kopit, John Eisner, Suzy Fay and Giovanna Sardelli, and to Philip Himberg, Lisa Peterson, Emily Bergl, Tommy Sadoski, and Naomi Peters for aiding me so much in the development of this play at the Sundance Theatre Lab. Final and warmest thanks to Sasha Eden, Victoria Pettibone, Josh Hecht, Tasha Gordon-Solomon, Jeremy Webb, Laura Heisler and Sean Dugan, without whom none of this would have happened.

BFF was given its World Premiere by WET (Women's Expressive Theater, Inc.) (Sasha Eden and Victoria Pettibone, Executive Producers) at The DR2 Theatre in New York City on February 24th, 2007. It was directed by Josh Hecht; the set design was by Robin Vest; the costume design was by Sara Jean Tosetti; the lighting design was by Clifton Taylor; the sound design and original music were by David Stephen Baker; the video projection design was by Kevin R. Frech; the production manager was David Nelson; the production stage manager was Ashley B. Delegal; the casting director was Jack Doulin; and the assistant producer was Ashley Eichhorn-Thompson. The cast was as follows:

LAUREN ................................................................ Sasha Eden
ELIZA .................................................................. Laura Heisler
SETH ................................................................... Jeremy Webb

# CHARACTERS

ELIZA, late 20s, early 30s
LAUREN, late 20s, early 30s
SETH, late 20s, early 30s

# PLACE

Upstate New York and New York City.

# TIME

1991 and 2005.

NOTE: Simple sets, quick scene changes, no intermission. It is also an option for Lauren to be offstage during Scene 12.

# BFF
## ("Best Friends Forever")

### Scene 1

*Lauren, twelve, is swimming in a pool. She gets out and dries herself off. Eliza, twelve, is lying on a towel, reading a magazine. It's summer; the sun is bright. Lauren is in a bikini. Eliza wears a T-shirt and eats, intermittently, from a box of cereal. Lauren lies down, her head on Eliza's stomach.*

LAUREN. Liza, what do you think it'll be like to be grown up?
ELIZA. I don't know.
LAUREN. I mean, do you think it feels different than this? *(Eliza thinks about it.)*
ELIZA. No. Probably not.
LAUREN. Right. Probably not.
ELIZA. Why do you ask?
LAUREN. I don't know.
ELIZA. Okay.
LAUREN. No, I mean, I just got this feeling, while I was swimming, that the years are gonna pass so quickly.
ELIZA. Oh … I don't want them to.
LAUREN. This feeling that everything happens at once, you know? That we're already grown up and walking around somewhere and doing some job and we just don't know it.
ELIZA. You're not making sense, Lauren.
LAUREN. I am.
ELIZA. Okay.
LAUREN. Let's make something up.
ELIZA. Okay.
LAUREN. Let's tell the future.
ELIZA. I don't want to think about the future.
LAUREN. Like, where are we gonna live in the year 2000?

7

ELIZA. I don't know —

LAUREN. New York City?

ELIZA. Yeah, I guess.

LAUREN. We could have, like, apartments next to each other.

ELIZA. *(Finally getting into it a little.)* We could live in the same apartment.

LAUREN. Absolutely. *(Beat.)* Will we get married?

ELIZA. To each other? hm

LAUREN. No! I meant, in general.

ELIZA. I think we will. When we want to.

LAUREN. How will we know when we want to?

ELIZA. I don't know. I guess when the right person comes along.

LAUREN. But who will the right person be?

ELIZA. Really nice.

LAUREN. Eliza.

ELIZA. What?

LAUREN. He's gotta be hot.

ELIZA. Of course hot. I meant hot too. Nice and hot.

LAUREN. And funny.

ELIZA. It would be great if he were funny. *(Beat.)* And he should have a secret.

LAUREN. What do you mean?

ELIZA. Something he only tells you.

LAUREN. I guess. Yeah.

ELIZA. He'll be shy but also open. A little awkward but in a sweet way.

LAUREN. If you say so.

ELIZA. Will you rub my back? *(Lauren does.)* Isn't this is a great day, Lauren?

LAUREN. It is.

ELIZA. I feel really happy right now.

LAUREN. You do?

ELIZA. I sort of wish we could just stay here forever.

LAUREN. We have til four, right? I mean, that's still a couple hours —

ELIZA. But I can feel it becoming a memory even as it's happening.

LAUREN. Don't say that.

ELIZA. But it's how I feel.

LAUREN. Hey, did you know that Jason Priestley lost twenty-five pounds?

ELIZA. I didn't.

LAUREN. Jason Priestley's so hot.

ELIZA. I know. Totally hot. *(Long beat.)* But do you ever get the feeling of missing someone even when you're sitting right next to them?

LAUREN. Liza —

ELIZA. I miss you. *(Beat.)*

LAUREN. I'm sorry.

ELIZA. About what?

LAUREN. I don't know.

## Scene 2

*Lauren, now in her late twenties, is doing yoga on a mat in a large empty room. Seth enters and stares at her for a few moments. He coughs. Lauren turns around. The two make eye contact for a long moment. Then Lauren begins to gather her things.*

SETH. You don't have to go.

LAUREN. Oh no, I was leaving anyway.

SETH. I think I'm just early for the next class.

LAUREN. I didn't know there was another class in here.

SETH. Yeah, there is. *(Beat.)* It has to do with finding your inner voice in a post 9/11 landscape.

LAUREN. Right.

SETH. I lost a bet.

LAUREN. *(Turning to leave.)* Okay.

SETH. But I figured maybe, well … given the way my life is now, it wouldn't be bad to try some new things. Why not try to find my inner voice? Find out if that sort of thing is possible.

LAUREN. What's the way your life is now?

SETH. I mean, maybe if more people had inner voices, the world would be in better shape.

LAUREN. I don't know.

SETH. *(Awkwardly.)* You look like you're in pretty good shape.

LAUREN. I have work.

SETH. My life now is a little monotonous. A little bit the same all the time.

LAUREN. I think that's what life's like.

SETH. I don't think it has to be.

LAUREN. You don't?

SETH. No. *(Beat.)*

LAUREN. Well. I better —

SETH. Right. *(Lauren heads for the door. Eliza's in the doorway.)* Um … what's your name? *(Eliza takes Lauren's hand and pulls her into the next scene. Seth doesn't see Eliza and watches Lauren go.)*

## Scene 3

*Lauren and Eliza, the teenagers, are singing karaoke in Lauren's bedroom. They're holding hands and dancing to a song like the Divinyls' "I Touch Myself."\* They're hamming it up. The song ends; they collapse on the floor.*

LAUREN. I think Mrs. Linklater should touch herself. She's so totally repressed.

ELIZA. Maybe all math teachers are.

LAUREN. Why, because numbers are like a language for people who don't want to use words?

ELIZA. No, because they all look totally repressed.

LAUREN. I bet Mrs. Linklater's a virgin.

ELIZA. I bet she is.

LAUREN. I bet she's never kissed anyone. I bet she lives alone and she's never smoked a cigarette. I bet she's having a very lonely summer.

ELIZA. Yeah, I bet.

LAUREN. Maybe she's an orphan and never knew any love and everything follows from that.

ELIZA. That's awful! … But yeah, maybe. I could see that.

LAUREN. I think my mom never slept with anyone but my dad.

---

\* See Special Note on Songs and Recordings on copyright page.

I asked her once … She told me it was none of my business. That's why I think it's true. *(Long beat.)* Oh, I'm sorry, Liza — I didn't mean to bring anything up —

ELIZA. No — it's fine.

LAUREN. I think you're doing so well these days. My mom says you seem to be doing really well and I think so too.

ELIZA. Sure, yeah. *(Long beat.)*

LAUREN. Anyway, sometimes I think my mom's shy and, like, modest, because her name is Sarah. I mean, isn't that a shy kind of name?

ELIZA. I don't know. Is my name shy?

LAUREN. No way. It's loud. It, like, has a voice. Eliza. I mean, say it.

ELIZA. Um, no.

LAUREN. Come on, say it … Eliza …

ELIZA. No.

LAUREN. Just say it. *(Then more dramatically.)* Eliza … *(Low and sexy.)* Eliza. Say it.

ELIZA. *(Snapping, angry.)* No!

LAUREN. *(Hurt.)* Okay. Sorry. *(Beat.)*

ELIZA. *(Quietly.)* You dweeb.

LAUREN. Lauren's quiet. I don't think she's shy but she's quiet. She slips along.

ELIZA. I think it's the other way around.

LAUREN. No. You're brave.

ELIZA. Right.

LAUREN. Your pick this time. *(Eliza leafs through the albums. She puts one on. It's slower and mellow. Her dad's favorite song. She stands, begins to sway.)* That's like … I don't know … I feel like my mom likes that song.

ELIZA. Right. No — I think I put it on by mistake. *(She stops it abruptly. She sits down. Beat.)* Lauren, do you ever feel like the hardest thing in the world is just waking up?

LAUREN. Wow, um … Liza?

ELIZA. What?

LAUREN. You know, the thing is, these days I'm never sure what you're going to say.

ELIZA. I surprise you?

LAUREN. Yeah, I mean. You do.

ELIZA. *(Thoughtfully.)* Good.

11

# Scene 4

*Lauren, the adult, is back on the yoga mat. Seth watches her again from the doorway.*

SETH. You must do this every Tuesday. *(Lauren turns around.)*
LAUREN. I guess that's the nature of a weekly class.
SETH. But you stay after.
LAUREN. I like quiet.
SETH. Me too.
LAUREN. *(Standing.)* So, did you find it?
SETH. What?
LAUREN. Your inner voice?
SETH. Oh. No. But I did learn some ways to begin to understand what an inner voice is. See, first you have to understand it, then you can begin to try to locate it. You can't try to find something when you don't know what you're looking for. It's all very …
LAUREN. What?
SETH. Well, I don't know you so I'm not sure how you feel about things like this. I could say "deep" with a sort of sarcastic edge or I could say it's all very zen and try to take it seriously. I don't want to offend you.
LAUREN. You're not offending me —
SETH. I don't want to make you late for work.
LAUREN. I'm always late.
SETH. What do you do?
LAUREN. I work with aquatic animals.
SETH. What, like at an aquarium?
LAUREN. No. *(Long beat.)*
SETH. Okay. *(Beat.)* I like your bracelets.
LAUREN. Thanks.
SETH. They caught my eye.
LAUREN. They were cheap.
SETH. Most people don't wear jewelry to work out, do they?
LAUREN. Right so what do you do?
SETH. Oh it's hard to explain. Very serious business. Lots of

abstract thinking and late nights.

LAUREN. Oh.

SETH. No — I'm kidding. I'm a banker. I mean, I work at a bank.

LAUREN. Are you married?

SETH. No. *(Beat.)* Are you?

LAUREN. I only asked because —

SETH. You think I'm coming on to you?

LAUREN. No, I … I don't know. Are you?

SETH. Can I?

LAUREN. I don't know, um —

SETH. Seth.

LAUREN. Right, Seth. I don't like invasions, you know.

SETH. Am I being invasive?

LAUREN. No, I'm just letting you know.

SETH. What's your name?

LAUREN. Eliza. hm

SETH. Eliza. I like it.

LAUREN. Did I say Eliza? I meant —

SETH. Eliza — like the song. *(Beat.)*

LAUREN. Is there a song?

SETH. I assume there are songs for most names. *(Long beat.)*

LAUREN. Well I don't think there's one for me.

SETH. Not yet, maybe. But these things get written every day, don't they?

LAUREN. I guess so.

# Scene 5

*Lauren and Eliza are on swings that have dropped down; the girls are too big for them, but they don't care. They hold hands.*

ELIZA. 1991. It doesn't sound like much, does it?

LAUREN. No.

ELIZA. No.

LAUREN. I wonder if we'll ever be a part of history, like real history. Like a war or a … revolution.

ELIZA. Maybe we don't want to be. My mom says things are better this way. Like you don't know to appreciate something until it's gone.

LAUREN. She's talking about your dad dying, right?

ELIZA. *(After a beat.)* I guess so, yeah.

LAUREN. But you appreciated him.

ELIZA. I don't know.

LAUREN. Liza, you did, you —

ELIZA. Anyway, the sixties would have been fun, right?

LAUREN. Totally fun.

ELIZA. Like, rad. *(Beat.)* Lauren?

LAUREN. Yeah? *(Beat.)*

ELIZA. Isn't this breeze great? Like peaceful?

LAUREN. Yeah.

ELIZA. Like we could be in the middle of nowhere at any point in history. Like people have been feeling this breeze for all of eternity. Like this could be August in 1891 or 1691 and we have no idea what's coming next even though it's all bound to happen; it'll happen no matter what, like space travel or women's rights; we're just, well, we're just in the middle of all this wind.

LAUREN. It's a really good breeze.

ELIZA. Sort of like we're outside of time.

LAUREN. I guess so. *(Beat. Lauren drops Eliza's hand.)* So I got my period.

ELIZA. What?

LAUREN. Yeah.

ELIZA. When?

LAUREN. Three days ago.

ELIZA. Oh.

LAUREN. It was annoying.

ELIZA. Oh.

LAUREN. My mom made me learn to use a tampon. Right away. She said there was no reason not to. But that was gross.

ELIZA. I can see why.

LAUREN. Can you?

ELIZA. Yeah.

LAUREN. I'm not sure it's something you can understand until you do it.

ELIZA. Well, I'm not sure if it's something I want to understand.

LAUREN. You don't even want to wear a bra yet.

ELIZA. Why should I?

LAUREN. Why not?
ELIZA. *(After a beat.)* So ... you still have it?
LAUREN. Yeah.
ELIZA. Like right now?
LAUREN. Yeah.
ELIZA. Gross.
LAUREN. Yeah.

## Scene 6

*Lauren and Seth are at a restaurant. They are silent and awkward for a few moments before speaking. Seth is drinking wine and Lauren has a cup of tea.*

SETH. So, I've heard it's not uncommon for soldiers in the heat of battle to become paralyzed with fear. Many get shot because they can't move. They're sitting ducks.
LAUREN. Gosh.
SETH. Right and the awful thing is, a lot of them, well, shit themselves as they're dying. Right when they're dying.
LAUREN. That is awful.
SETH. I know. *(Beat, then trying to be funny.)* Death, right? It's just no fun. *(Awkward beat.)* But war's really just survival of the fittest. And the thing is there's no way to train for it. You just get into the situation and then you react that way or you don't. You can't simulate war.
LAUREN. No. *(Beat.)*
SETH. So do you have to be like a really good swimmer to be a marine biologist?
LAUREN. Decent, I guess.
SETH. Uh-huh.
LAUREN. I mean, you have to like the water.
SETH. Right. *(Beat.)*
LAUREN. Do you like your wine?
SETH. It's good.
LAUREN. Good.

SETH. *(Referring to her teacup.)* Do you like your — ?

LAUREN. Yeah.

SETH. Good.

LAUREN. So —

SETH. Right, I mean, my dad — my father — was drafted for Vietnam. He got a bad number in the lottery — twenty-two — and he was drafted. But he never saw action. He was sent to type code in a dark room in the jungle. Once he heard gun shots, but that was all.

LAUREN. So he was lucky.

SETH. I guess so.

LAUREN. I could never go to war.

SETH. Neither could I. But you never know. I mean, the way we're living, you think nothing will happen but then the next moment, it does. It will … Like, my buddy Trevor was in Tower Two on 9/11 for a meeting; I mean he's all right; he wasn't very high up, but … things just, they don't wait for you. They happen anyway. They creep up on you and take over your life so that you don't ever, well, fully recover. *(Beat.)*

LAUREN. What happened?

SETH. To Trevor? He was okay — he just, well, got down in time.

LAUREN. No, to you.

SETH. What do you mean?

LAUREN. You don't have to talk about it.

SETH. Did I … Was I suggesting something?

LAUREN. I think so.

SETH. It must be unconscious.

LAUREN. Okay.

SETH. No, it's just that … well, my dad died.

LAUREN. Oh.

SETH. I mean, it's nothing. It was a year ago. It was a long time ago now.

LAUREN. That's not a long time.

SETH. Let's just … let's change the subject. Ask me something. Anything.

LAUREN. Are you sure?

SETH. I'm totally not hung up on it, just so you know. I'm not one of those —

LAUREN. Seth —

SETH. Like self-pitying, moaning, "Oh I have dreams and they torment me," analysis every afternoon kind of … well, that's just not me.

LAUREN.  I didn't think it was. *(Lauren reaches out without meaning to and touches his hair. Seth is shocked. She pulls her hand back. Beat.)*

SETH.  Well, he died of lung cancer. Never even smoked a cigarette.

LAUREN.  Wow.

SETH.  I'm ruining this, aren't I? Am I ruining this?

LAUREN.  No.

SETH.  Anyway, I'm totally not … I mean I barely ever think of it anymore.

LAUREN.  It would be normal if you did —

SETH.  So, ask me something — just ask me about something else.

LAUREN.  What should I ask?

SETH.  My dad had a mustache. In the past year, I've tried growing them, but on me, they don't look right, like I'm impersonating a much older or much different man.

LAUREN.  Tell me.

SETH.  What?

LAUREN.  Did you think of me at all today? At work?

SETH.  Wow. That's quite a question … Wow. But since you asked … I mean that is quite a question. But I guess … yes. Yes I did.

LAUREN.  In what way?

SETH.  Well, I was nervous about tonight.

LAUREN.  You were nervous?

SETH.  I worried. I'm a worrier. I try to plan what to say and then it never comes out right. I've learned to stop writing out conversations though and focus on topics, ad lib from there.

LAUREN.  So your story about working at that animal shelter?

SETH.  Vaguely planned.

LAUREN.  And your mother becoming a dentist?

SETH.  Definitely planned. You don't see many women making mid-career moves into dental hygiene.

LAUREN.  You said you like to walk in the rain.

SETH.  I do. But I knew I'd talk about it. It makes women think I'm serious and potentially romantic.

LAUREN.  What else do you worry about?

SETH.  I worry I might clam up at any moment around you.

LAUREN.  I *am* very intimidating.

SETH.  Yes, Eliza, you are. *(Beat.)* But do you think —

LAUREN.  What?

SETH. I wouldn't usually ask this kind of question. I mean, usually I'd wait to see if it would happen organically.

LAUREN. What?

SETH. I was wondering if … Eliza … do you think I could take you home tonight? *(Long beat.)*

LAUREN. I don't think so.

SETH. Why not?

LAUREN. It's a story.

SETH. You don't like me. I knew it.

LAUREN. No, it's just — I should tell you —

SETH. Well, do you like me?

LAUREN. I don't think I know you yet.

SETH. But you must have a sense. You must know whether you might.

LAUREN. I might.

● **Scene 7**

*Lauren and Eliza sit on a dock by a lake. Summer's ending; school's about to begin.*

ELIZA. I think he's kind of goofy-looking.

LAUREN. Are you serious?

ELIZA. I mean, isn't his new haircut kind of … weird? Is it supposed to stick up like that?

LAUREN. I think so.

ELIZA. Well, I think it's weird. Like an alien.

LAUREN. He's not like an alien.

ELIZA. No, just his hair.

LAUREN. Well, I like it.

ELIZA. I know. *(Beat. Lauren dips her toes in the water.)*

LAUREN. Remember when I went with Julie and Jason to that field up near her dad's place?

ELIZA. Where was I?

LAUREN. You didn't want to come that day.

ELIZA. I don't remember that.

LAUREN. And we saw this cow but Julie thought it might be a bull and we didn't know what to do so we all just walked really slowly towards the fence, hoping it wouldn't follow us.

ELIZA. Julie's a cow.

LAUREN. The whole time I was staring at it and it was staring at me and I couldn't look away, Liza. I couldn't look away.

ELIZA. Wasn't Julie just jabbering away? She never stops talking.

LAUREN. I mean, in the end, it *was* just a cow. It was fine. Jason laughed at me because I was so scared. But seriously, I thought I might die and I think he did too.

ELIZA. Once I thought I might —

LAUREN. It felt like it would never let me go but I also didn't want it to. Like, I could have stared into its eyes forever.

ELIZA. When my mom left me at home at Halloween last year and the intercom light kept flashing as though someone was in another room of the house, I was pretty terrified.

LAUREN. But it's not the same. I'm talking about something primal. Like … lust.

ELIZA. *(Not understanding.)* Okay.

LAUREN. I mean, I know you were scared.

ELIZA. I don't like staying alone to begin with. I mean, when I'm alone it feels like there's no one else and there's nothing to come. Does that ever happen to you?

LAUREN. Not really, no.

ELIZA. Oh, well, I think I'm exaggerating. And I mean, anyway, I can just stay with you. It's easier and I'm not scared that way … BFF, right?

LAUREN. *(They pinky swear.)* BFF. But I do really think he's cute. I like his hair now. *(Beat.)* And I think Ben's cute too. Do you think Ben's cute?

ELIZA. No.

LAUREN. I think so. And I thought when we ran into them he was looking at you.

ELIZA. He wasn't.

LAUREN. He was. I noticed.

ELIZA. He had something stuck between his teeth, like a seed or something. I noticed that.

LAUREN. That's not the point.

ELIZA. Is there a point here?

LAUREN. The point is, you should go for him.

ELIZA. Well that would imply that I want to go for someone.

LAUREN. Don't you?

ELIZA. No!

LAUREN. Okay, okay …

ELIZA. I just think it's gross … I think we're too young to be thinking of stuff like that. That's what my mom says!

LAUREN. Don't get worked up, Liza.

ELIZA. I'm not worked up.

LAUREN. But you think there's something wrong with my liking Jason?

ELIZA. Just do what you want.

LAUREN. Well, I will. *(Beat.)*

ELIZA. So what do you want to do now?

LAUREN. I don't know. I think I'm gonna go for a swim.

ELIZA. You want me to just sit here and watch you swim?

LAUREN. You could swim with me.

ELIZA. Ha ha.

LAUREN. It's really not scary, Liza. I mean, I love it. It, like, takes you away from everything.

ELIZA. Really?

LAUREN. Someday you'll try it.

ELIZA. I don't think so.


# Scene 8


*Lauren and Seth are at a dance lesson. They're dancing in each other's arms.*


SETH. I knew you'd be good at this and I'd be awful.

LAUREN. You're not awful.

SETH. I guess I had this optimistic idea that we'd, like, learn something together, at the same pace, but …

LAUREN. I used to take lessons. All the kids took ballroom dance one winter. This old man taught it and he was traditional, like he made the men ask the women to dance with them. We were twelve. It was horrific.

SETH. I bet you were always asked.

LAUREN. No.

SETH. I don't believe it.

LAUREN. How about you? What were you like?

SETH. What do you mean?

LAUREN. I mean, did people find you attractive, when you were young?

SETH. Oh. I don't know. I guess I was average.

LAUREN. You weren't average.

SETH. I wasn't?

LAUREN. No.

SETH. Thanks. *(Beat.)* Or did you mean I was below average? *(Lauren punches him playfully.)*

LAUREN. So when was the first time you —

SETH. What?

LAUREN. Like, went out with someone.

SETH. I went out with Hannah Carerra in sixth grade but I don't think that counts.

LAUREN. Why not?

SETH. Well … it was a yearlong relationship and in that year we went out three times. Once to Burger King, where my older brother chaperoned and made fun of us at the same time. Once for breakfast where we ran into my mom's friend and she sat with us. And once to a dance, where we never even touched.

LAUREN. I think that counts. *(Beat.)*

SETH. So what about you? When was the first time you went out with someone?

LAUREN. Oh. Um. I guess there was this guy Jason.

SETH. Jason, huh? And what was he like?

LAUREN. Short. I guess. His voice cracked all the time so it sounded like he was making fun of himself.

SETH. Yeah, I matured late too. My voice didn't change til like twelfth grade.

LAUREN. It still cracks a little every now and then.

SETH. Because I'm not entirely grown up, right? I like to think the kid I was still creeps in sometimes.

LAUREN. That's a sweet idea. *(Beat.)*

SETH. So tell me something about you. Something I don't know.

LAUREN. Like what?

SETH. I know you don't want me to pry. But give me something.

21

LAUREN. Um.

SETH. You can do it.

LAUREN. I'm embarrassed.

SETH. Choose not to be embarrassed … It's just me, after all.

LAUREN. It's you.

SETH. Right.

LAUREN. Well … I love to swim.

SETH. Why?

LAUREN. Because it's like you're on another planet where the things that were once useful don't matter anymore — doing math, or making friends, or getting to work on time. You just have to focus on being. Because it feels like time isn't passing.

SETH. That's nice.

LAUREN. It is?

SETH. I think we all look for ways to escape it. Time, I mean.

LAUREN. We do?

SETH. Yeah. Some people sleep too much, or drink. I daydream, pretend I'm a kid again.

LAUREN. Me too!

SETH. I picture me and my brother and my dad in the car, just driving. We're not going anywhere, we're just driving. And the radio's on and time is … well, it's … it hasn't gotten to us yet. And there's the open road and my brother complains about the radio station and I don't care. I just let him change it.

LAUREN. It's so sad.

SETH. What?

LAUREN. That you can't just stay in the car.

SETH. I don't think so. *(Seth kisses Lauren. It's quick and Lauren pulls away. Eliza appears. They keep dancing for a while before Lauren notices Eliza; when she does, she's shocked.)* Oh, you're stepping on my feet!

LAUREN. Sorry!

SETH. I didn't mean we had to stop.

LAUREN. I hate dancing.

SETH. You okay, Liza?

LAUREN. Oh God.

SETH. Liza? *(She stares at Eliza and Eliza stares at her.)*

22

*Irelyn drag in table SR* — *[handwritten]*

*E* — *[handwritten, top right]*

# • Scene 9

*Lauren and Eliza. After a school dance.*

*Slump in chair* — *[handwritten]*

LAUREN. And then he tongue-kissed me.

ELIZA. Really? *'fascinated'* *Sit up* — *[handwritten]*

LAUREN. And it felt … strange and wet and slimy … but nice.

ELIZA. Then what happened? *"suspense"* — *[handwritten]*

LAUREN. Well, that's it.

ELIZA. That's it?

LAUREN. We did that for a while and then he kind of patted my shoulder, maybe he was aiming for my arm, and went back on the dance floor.

ELIZA. So you'll see him again?

LAUREN. I don't know. I guess so.

ELIZA. He didn't say, like, "let's do this again"?

LAUREN. No. *→ Stand XSL* — *[handwritten]*

ELIZA. Jerk. I mean that's really unimpressive.

LAUREN. I think he's shy.

ELIZA. Not too shy to stick his tongue down your throat.

LAUREN. Eliza!

ELIZA. What?

LAUREN. Don't be vulgar.

ELIZA. So now you're mad at me? *→ sarcasm/confused* — *[handwritten]*

LAUREN. Maybe, I don't know. I wanted to tell you and you —

ELIZA. What? What did I do? *genuine* *Start walking to chair Ire.* — *[handwritten]*

LAUREN. You didn't understand. *(Beat.)* I mean, why didn't you dance with Ben when he asked you?

ELIZA. Ew. How can you even ask that?

LAUREN. I mean, he's cute *→ Walk away SL, arms crossed trying to escape* — *[handwritten]*

ELIZA. No he's not!

LAUREN. And he likes you.

ELIZA. I hate the kind of dancing everyone does, the kind you do with Jason. It's way too, like, close.

LAUREN. Why don't you just dance with him next time? I bet he'll still ask you. Julie doesn't think he'll hold a grudge.

23

LIZA. I don't care what Julie thinks.

LAUREN. You can dance with him in any way you want.

ELIZA. Um, no thank you.

LAUREN. But why not, Liza? *(Eliza stands and dances.)* What are you doing?

ELIZA. I'm dancing to my own beat.

LAUREN. I don't get it.

ELIZA. There's nothing to get.

LAUREN. You're kind of exasperating, you know that?

ELIZA. Thanks.

LAUREN. No, I mean, I just think you could try a little harder to understand what I'm dealing with right now.

ELIZA. Maybe you could try to understand what I'm dealing with.

LAUREN. What's that?

ELIZA. Exactly.

LAUREN. Liza —

ELIZA. You want me to dance with Ben and then let him do things to me so that I'll understand what you're dealing with?

LAUREN. I mean, is this about your dad, Liza?

ELIZA. I'm sorry?

LAUREN. My mom says it might take a long time for you to, like, fully recover. So now you're just still really upset about it, right?

ELIZA. I don't know what you're talking about.

LAUREN. I'm just saying maybe you have a thing about guys because you don't have a dad.

ELIZA. That's an awful thing to say.

LAUREN. But is it true?

ELIZA. No.

LAUREN. I've heard that girls who grow up without fathers can be really repressed when it comes to sexuality.

ELIZA. I'm not repressed.

LAUREN. Yes, you are.

ELIZA. What makes you think that?

LAUREN. Everything.

ELIZA. Look, I don't want to talk about my dad.

LAUREN. I'm talking about you.

ELIZA. Well, what do I have to do to prove to you that I'm not repressed, huh? Bring my dad back to life?

LAUREN. No.

24

ELIZA. Fuck some guy?

LAUREN. Eliza! No.

ELIZA. Lose twenty pounds and waltz around in miniskirts and halter tops like some sluts I know?

LAUREN. Are you talking about me?

ELIZA. Ding ding, Einstein. You know, you're lucky you're pretty because intelligence really isn't your strong suit. *(Eliza storms out.)*


## Scene 10


*Lauren paces in front of a park bench. She's waiting. She's been waiting for a long time. Seth appears.*


LAUREN. Seth!

SETH. I'm so sorry. I have a tremendous excuse — the trains and the — I got lost; it took longer than I thought; there were delays —

LAUREN. What kind of delays? I mean, it's been half an hour ... I thought —

SETH. I'm sorry —

LAUREN. I thought you'd been hit by a bus ... I thought a building had blown up. I thought some awful disease had been released in the subways and you were coughing up blood crouched in some sad little corner!

SETH. No ... I just ...

LAUREN. What?

SETH. I lost track of time.

LAUREN. You forgot about me?

SETH. No. I mean ... I didn't. I had this all planned out. Look — *(He holds up a basket.)* Wine, and cheese and crackers and grapes. I mean, I brought grapes! We can feed each other grapes!

LAUREN. I thought you were gone.

SETH. I'm right here.

LAUREN. This is ridiculous.

SETH. What is?

LAUREN. Worrying. Thinking you were gone. It's ridiculous.

SETH. No — it's okay to worry. It's fine. It's like my middle name.

25

It's like home to me. Like the living-room couch.

LAUREN. I don't like it.

SETH. It's normal. It means you like me. *(Beat.)* I'm sorry. I didn't mean to make you wait. It was the last thing I wanted.

LAUREN. I was thinking.

SETH. About me? About us? Because I don't want this minor, this — I'm not usually late. It won't become a pattern —

LAUREN. No, about other things. Like, life.

SETH. Oh.

LAUREN. How predictable it is.

SETH. You mean, you knew I'd be late? *I* didn't know I'd be late —

LAUREN. I just … I never thought I'd … be in this kind of situation.

SETH. What kind of situation?

LAUREN. You know. Like, with you. I mean, I never honestly thought I'd be, like … seriously into —

SETH. What are you trying to tell me?

LAUREN. It's such a beautiful day, isn't it? This breeze, and … I mean, I feel like I could be sitting here at any time in the history of the world.

SETH. Eliza —

LAUREN. Don't you ever feel that we're just on the edge of our lives? That they're happening but we're outside of them and nothing we can do will stop anything?

SETH. Like fate.

LAUREN. Like being stuck. Even if we know what the right thing to do is, we still won't do it. There's something we can't define holding us back.

SETH. That's a pretty negative outlook.

LAUREN. Sometimes I can be negative. You do know that, right? That I can be negative? I'm not as easygoing as you are.

SETH. I'm not easygoing.

LAUREN. You seem it. Easy to get to know.

SETH. Those aren't the same thing.

LAUREN. It's just that … I don't think I'm as simple as I've seemed. Or something like that. I mean, we've just been having a good time together and I'm not like that. I don't just have a good time. There are consequences.

SETH. Are the consequences bad? You make them sound bad.

LAUREN. Yes. They're bad.

SETH. I don't know what you're talking about. I think you're great and that's all that matters.

LAUREN. Don't say that.

SETH. Listen, we don't have to do the grapes and the ... maybe ... do you want a hot dog? There's a Gray's Papaya not too far from the park and I love their hot dogs ... something about them. I don't know what it is —

LAUREN. No, I don't want a hot dog.

SETH. Okay. *(Beat.)* It was just an idea.

LAUREN. I'm just feeling so ...

SETH. Frustrated?

LAUREN. No! Not frustrated. Aren't you listening to me? I'm trying to express something to you.

SETH. I'm sorry, I'm —

LAUREN. Yeah, well I'm sorry too. I'm sorry too.

SETH. What do you want me to say?

LAUREN. I don't know. I think I want to be alone.

SETH. Well, maybe you should be alone.

LAUREN. Right. Maybe I should be.


● **Scene 11**


*Lauren and Eliza sit on the floor; it's raining out. Autumn and boredom.*


ELIZA. We could play cards.

LAUREN. No.

ELIZA. Prank phone calls?

LAUREN. No.

ELIZA. Monopoly?

LAUREN. Ew. No.

ELIZA. I'd like to take a walk in the rain.

LAUREN. I know. You and your walks.

ELIZA. I get thinking done in the rain.

LAUREN. Why won't he call?

ELIZA. When I say thinking I don't mean like concrete thoughts.

I mean, it's totally abstract. Like I'll just picture things, scenes from my life. I just replay scenes from my life.

LAUREN. I left a message over fourteen hours ago.

ELIZA. I think it's fifteen by now.

LAUREN. Great. Fifteen.

ELIZA. Lauren I'm sorry I called you a slut.

LAUREN. It's okay.

ELIZA. It is?

LAUREN. I'm more focused on other things right now anyway.

ELIZA. Oh. Well, I think we should try to get your mind off —

LAUREN. I don't want to get my mind off it. I want him to call.

ELIZA. Lauren.

LAUREN. What?

ELIZA. Lauren. *(Eliza puts her hand on Lauren's shoulder.)*

LAUREN. What? *(Eliza puts her arms around Lauren's shoulders —* *maternal.)* What are you doing?

ELIZA. I'm giving you a hug.

LAUREN. Why?

ELIZA. You seem to need some consolation. I'm doing my best. *(Lauren wriggles away.)*

LAUREN. I'm fine.

ELIZA. You're not acting fine.

LAUREN. I'm not?

ELIZA. No. *(Beat.)*

LAUREN. Last night I had a dream that my boobs grew and I was like a 38 double D.

ELIZA. Was that a nightmare?

LAUREN. No! … I was so happy. *(Beat.)* And what if I told you I've been … fantasizing.

ELIZA. Fantasizing about what?

LAUREN. You know.

ELIZA. No.

LAUREN. About Jason, about …

ELIZA. Oh no, ew. Don't tell me.

LAUREN. Yeah. I feel … kind of awful. Like, dirty.

ELIZA. That is *not* normal.

LAUREN. It isn't?

ELIZA. No.

LAUREN. It's like, when I see him, I want things. And when I go to sleep at night, I want the same things only … they're more intense then, when I'm on my own.

ELIZA. I think you should try to stop thinking.

LAUREN. How?

ELIZA. Think about other stuff. Think about … me. Like, my mom's driving to the mall tomorrow and we could go with her.

LAUREN. To do what? Buy towels?

ELIZA. Faucets. I think. For the kitchen sink.

LAUREN. Why won't he call?

ELIZA. But we could hang out. We could see a movie. While she shops. You know she takes forever.

LAUREN. Maybe I didn't adopt the right tone. "Just give me a call when you have a chance" could sound a little like it doesn't expect a response. Is that true? Or?

ELIZA. When you call me and say that, I call you back.

LAUREN. But that's you.

ELIZA. I know.

LAUREN. I mean, he's probably busy. Maybe his dad like took him out of town or something.

ELIZA. Or maybe he doesn't like you.

LAUREN. What?

ELIZA. It is possible.

LAUREN. What do you mean?

ELIZA. That he's not interested in you. It does happen.

LAUREN. But I've put so much time into liking him.

ELIZA. I know.

LAUREN. He likes me. Come on … doesn't he?

ELIZA. I don't know. I can't say for sure. It's not like he's called you back.

LAUREN. You know, Julie Miller says you're a prude.

ELIZA. What?

LAUREN. Yeah.

ELIZA. Why would she say that? I don't even know her.

LAUREN. Because I told her you are. I told her you don't like anyone. *(Beat.)*

ELIZA. You did that?

LAUREN. I just wanted another opinion. I can't do everything on my own.

ELIZA. You told her? You went behind my back?

LAUREN. I guess I did. Sorry.

ELIZA. Sorry? No, I mean … why?

29

LAUREN. Now everyone kind of knows. I guess Julie has a big mouth.

ELIZA. She's known for that.

LAUREN. I guess so. So now you kind of like have to prove that you're not.

ELIZA. Are you making this up?

LAUREN. Come on. I don't lie.

ELIZA. Well, I'm not proving anything.

LAUREN. It's just that … Julie thinks you might be holding me back.

ELIZA. If holding you back means keeping you sane.

LAUREN. To be honest, she doesn't know why we're friends.

ELIZA. Well, did you tell her?

LAUREN. No.

ELIZA. Why not?

LAUREN. Why are we friends? I mean … *(Beat.)*

ELIZA. Did you hear what you just said?

LAUREN. I didn't mean it.

ELIZA. You're sorry?

LAUREN. I'm sorry. *(The phone rings.)*


# Scene 12


*Lauren is at a small desk in front of a mirror. On the other side of the stage, Seth holds a guitar. He begins to play; he's teaching himself. He has a* How to Play Guitar *manual on his lap. He tries different chords. He suddenly reaches for the phone and dials. Lauren's phone rings.*


SETH. Eliza, please pick up the phone. Please. I'm sorry I left you alone. I guess when people say they want to be alone what they really mean is they want to be with other people and I read that all wrong. Please pick up. I mean, I went out with some friends last night and Trevor told this story about a date he had. He met this girl online. Apparently they match perfectly in terms of goals and lifestyle, whatever that means. He says I should go online too, Liza.

Meet someone. I say I'm already taken. At that point, my friends all laugh. They shoot each other knowing glances. They say, "Seth, you're a real romantic, aren't you;" they say I went on a few dates and now I think I'm married. And considering the fact that I haven't heard from you, maybe they're right that I thought we were … closer than we were. So given all that, I've made a sort of promise to myself. I say sort of because it might be hard to stick to but I think I should and so does Nancy — my therapist, I mean. She thinks, and I mean, I agree, that this should be the last message I leave you. It's a very one-sided relationship I'm engaged in, she says, and I guess she's right. So when I hang up I'm not calling back. I mean, I'll call back if you call me first and leave a message. I'm just not going to leave any more of these … whatever these are. But before I go … I just want to say … well, maybe this is my last chance, so why the hell not, right? I mean, I think I was starting to … I mean, you might not know it, but I'm not a real hotshot with women; I don't date that much. But I've dated enough … I mean, I've met enough women to know that you're really very … I mean, I think you're something. Really something. And for what it's worth, whatever it is you're going through right now … we can get through it. It'll be okay. I mean I *know* in my gut that if we're together, we can … But anyway I guess I'll leave it there. So, well, goodbye. I'm hanging up now. And I won't beg you to call me back … but why not just call me back? *(He hangs up and sits with the guitar without playing.)*

## Scene 13

*Lauren is applying makeup in front of a mirror while Eliza watches, chomping loudly on carrot sticks.*

LAUREN.  I mean, it's not like he could expect me to buy a new dress, right? My mom was like if you really need one Lauren but it'll be an early birthday present and do you really want that? And I don't want that. I don't want to cut into my birthday present. It's just that, well, Julie thinks I look fat in pink and I should really

Julie is
a bitch, lol

31

have a cute little black dress. She says everyone should have a little black cocktail dress. It says so in *Mademoiselle*, so it must be true. On the other hand, why not be a little different, right? I'm torn. I mean, I don't want to just blend in. Hey, can you give me a hand here? *(Eliza stands and helps Lauren with her mascara.)* Thanks. I mean, do you think my lashes are too long? I want it to look like I'm wearing makeup but not nearly as much as I'm actually wearing. On the other hand, should it look like I'm wearing it at all? Jason went out with Maggie before me and she never wore any makeup because she has like perfect skin. What a whore. *(Eliza eats carrots.)* Aren't you going to say anything?

ELIZA. No.

LAUREN. When are you going to get ready?

ELIZA. Do you think carrots are kind of phallic?

LAUREN. I think everything's kind of phallic; now shouldn't you get ready? We're leaving in two hours.

ELIZA. I'm well-acquainted with the time.

LAUREN. There's no need to be snide.

ELIZA. I don't think I'm going.

LAUREN. Oh perfume! We need perfume! *(She runs around frantically looking for some.)* Do you know where it is?

ELIZA. Did you hear me? I said I'm not going.

LAUREN. I heard you.

ELIZA. Okay then.

LAUREN. The thing is, I don't really believe you. I'm sure you'll change your mind. I think this is some ploy either to make me feel sorry for you or stay home with you and you know what? I'm not your babysitter, Liza. I'm just not.

ELIZA. Wow. *(She stands, she claps.)*

LAUREN. What are you doing?

ELIZA. Are you sure you don't have anything to add?

LAUREN. What do you mean?

ELIZA. Cuz I'd love to hear more.

LAUREN. Look, Liza — I think maybe … I mean, I've been thinking about it, and maybe it's true what Julie says.

ELIZA. What does Julie say now?

LAUREN. She thinks maybe we need some time apart.

ELIZA. Excuse me?

LAUREN. Like this whole thing about your not coming tonight. Maybe you shouldn't come. You don't like these things anyway. I could go without you.

ELIZA. You could?

LAUREN. Yeah. I think so. Yeah. And like, what if I smoke a cigarette or something? Or God forbid have a drink? You'll go apeshit and I don't want to risk offending you. I understand your point of view but you should understand mine and maybe just politely back out. No one will judge you.

ELIZA. Are you kidding? Everyone will judge me!

LAUREN. No — no, I don't think so.

ELIZA. What are you saying?

LAUREN. I'm just saying I don't think you should come tonight … and maybe later this week we should skip certain things.

ELIZA. Like what?

LAUREN. Like … everything. Like maybe I do want some time alone.

ELIZA. Not alone. With Julie. And with Jason. *(Beat, then putting down the carrots, and quietly:)* Don't do this, okay.

LAUREN. What? I didn't quite hear you.

ELIZA. I said, don't do this.

LAUREN. Do what?

ELIZA. Abandon me.

LAUREN. It's not abandoning … it's just … taking a break. *(Eliza begins to cry. She tries to hide it but can't. It's been building.)*

ELIZA. Don't. Please don't.

LAUREN. Why are you crying?

ELIZA. *(Her tone sharper and volume raised.)* Why do you think?

LAUREN. Don't just yell at me like that! I mean, I'm trying to have a conversation with you!

ELIZA. I'm not yelling.

LAUREN. You were.

ELIZA. Okay … well, what if I just go to the damn dance? Let's just do that. I don't want to go but I will — I'll go.

LAUREN. Honestly, I think it's too late for that.

ELIZA. No. I mean, I'll go. I'll get dressed. Let me get dressed right now. *(She starts taking her clothes off.)*

LAUREN. Ew. What are you doing?

ELIZA. I'm getting changed. What does it look like I'm doing?

LAUREN. I don't really want to see your whole body.

ELIZA. God! What can I do? What do you want me to do? *(Beat.)*

LAUREN. This is about your dad, isn't it …

BRO WTF

ELIZA. What are you talking about? Lauren, please … *(Eliza tries to touch Lauren, to hug her.)*
LAUREN. Get off me.
ELIZA. No. Lauren, please.
LAUREN. *(Getting away from her.)* I'm sorry your dad died. But … it's not really an excuse for …
ELIZA. What?
LAUREN. I mean, it's kind of obvious.
ELIZA. What?
LAUREN. I mean, you're like a lesbian, right? *(Beat. Eliza looks down at herself, half-naked, and then at Lauren.)* Right? I mean, everyone says so. Julie says girls without father figures are much more likely to … go that route.
ELIZA. Lauren.
LAUREN. I just don't know why you didn't tell me.
ELIZA. Tell you …
LAUREN. So you're just gonna cry like a baby? Like a little kid?
ELIZA. *(Crumpling to the floor.)* Lauren.
LAUREN. I mean, I'm really sick of all this crying all the time. I can't take care of you anymore, Liza. I just, I have other things to do.
ELIZA. *(Still looking at Lauren.)* Lauren.
LAUREN. I mean, you just didn't understand. I'm sorry but it's not my fault that you don't like Ben. You just have to accept the fact that I do like Jason and we're together and I want certain things and — *(She begins to leave.)*
ELIZA. Where are you going?
LAUREN. To the dance with my boyfriend. To have a good time for once. Okay? *(Lauren looks at her and exits. Eliza holds herself.)*
Bitch

## Scene 14

*Lauren and Seth are at a bar.*

LAUREN. I'm so glad you could come out. I know it was last minute.
SETH. That's okay.

LAUREN.  I mean, at least I suggested a bar near the bank, right?
SETH.  I guess.
LAUREN.  I'm sorry it's kind of well, seedy. That's what you get when you find a bar online, right?
SETH.  Right.
LAUREN.  I really wanted to see you, Seth.
SETH.  Uh-huh.
LAUREN.  Here, let's have a drink. Should we have a drink?
SETH.  Okay.
LAUREN.  What do you want?
SETH.  What are you having?
LAUREN.  I don't know. Something strong. Absinthe? Um, is that imported here yet?
SETH.  Eliza —
LAUREN.  I missed you. And I wanted to see you. And I'm sorry I didn't call you back. I feel awful. I mean, I know I'm awful. I don't know what's wrong with me.
SETH.  I left you five messages. Embarrassing messages.
LAUREN.  I don't like when things feel inevitable. I want to see if they'll endure despite certain obstacles.
SETH.  Like a week of ignoring me.
LAUREN.  I guess.
SETH.  I just don't know if I understand you — *(She kisses him suddenly.)* Is that an apology?
LAUREN.  It's … Seth, I need to tell you something —
SETH.  What?
LAUREN.  See, I'm not — *(Before she can finish, he kisses her.)*
SETH.  Not what? Not gonna do that to me, ever again?
LAUREN.  Right. Right.
SETH.  Good. It wasn't any fun. I'd say it ranks just ahead of the week I had my wisdom teeth out and just behind the week at the bank last year when they made us wear berets.
LAUREN.  Berets?
SETH.  Gimmicks don't generally work and that one was no exception.
LAUREN.  I'm really sorry, Seth.
SETH.  *(Genuinely.)* It wasn't as bad as the week when my dad died.
LAUREN.  I'm sure it wasn't.
SETH.  Anyway.
LAUREN.  Tell me what your dad was like.

SETH. I think it's better not to talk about it, better to be distracted.
LAUREN. No! I mean … no. I think it's bad to keep things bottled up.
SETH. Are you sure?
LAUREN. Yes.

## Scene 15

*A couple months have passed. Lauren and Seth are in bed together. It's morning. They're reading the paper. Lauren's eating cereal from a box.*

LAUREN. I can't decide if I want to read or go back to sleep.
SETH. Go back to sleep. The news'll wait.
LAUREN. I know. But it's nice, reading next to you.
SETH. It is nice.
LAUREN. Give me something to read. Something you think I'll like.
SETH. Okay. *(He leafs through the paper.)* Here. *(He hands a section to Lauren.)*
LAUREN. Is this some kind of joke?
SETH. Sort of.
LAUREN. Well, I don't get it. I mean, obituaries?
SETH. I want us to appreciate things.
LAUREN. Oh.
SETH. Because, I mean, I really do appreciate things, these days. I appreciate you.
LAUREN. Oh.
SETH. And it's good to remind ourselves, sometimes. That everything's transient.
LAUREN. *(Snippily.)* I don't need to be reminded of that.
SETH. You know, you never agree with me.
LAUREN. What?
SETH. I mean, why can't you ever agree with me?
LAUREN. I do agree with you. All the time.
SETH. There you go again.

36

LAUREN. Seth —

SETH. Sometimes it feels like you're just out to contradict me. And/or make me feel like an idiot but I like to think it's less vindictive than that.

LAUREN. You think I'm vindictive? *(Lauren gets out of bed, paces.)*

SETH. What are you doing?

LAUREN. Torturing myself.

SETH. Why?

LAUREN. It's who I am.

SETH. Come here. *(She doesn't go to him.)* You know, Trevor's screensaver is this one line scrolling across. It's Shakespeare, you know: "Our remedies oft in ourselves do lie" and I was thinking about it yesterday when I should have been working, and I realized that it's true, that we do, like, have the power to make ourselves happy.

LAUREN. I don't think we do, Seth.

SETH. Of course we do.

LAUREN. No. Once I was swimming; I was in the ocean — this was during college — and I dove down so deep and the water was so clear at the bottom and so beautiful, like hauntingly beautiful, that I almost didn't go back up.

SETH. But you did go back up.

LAUREN. I mean, you feel your lungs get tight.

SETH. You saved yourself.

LAUREN. I could have not saved myself.

SETH. I'd save you, if I could.

LAUREN. You would?

SETH. Yes. *(Beat.)*

LAUREN. So maybe we'll go swimming one day? I think I'd like to swim with you.

SETH. And I'd love to see you in a bikini.

LAUREN. No —

SETH. Or we could go skinny-dipping —

LAUREN. Seth, I'm being serious.

SETH. Yes, of course we can go swimming, Liza.

LAUREN. But Eliza's scared of the water.

SETH. What?

LAUREN. I mean, when I was a baby I fell in a pool and almost drowned and ever since then —

SETH. What are you talking about? What's going on?

LAUREN. Please don't leave me.

SETH. Look at me. I'm not going anywhere.

LAUREN. Seth?

SETH. I'm not going anywhere. But can you try to explain to me what's going on with you? Because in these moments, I'm confused. I don't have a handle on ... I worry you won't ever —

LAUREN. What?

SETH. Because it's not about meeting your parents, or seeing your office. I don't even care that you don't want to hang out with Trevor. He can be annoying sometimes.

LAUREN. I'm sorry, Seth —

SETH. It's just that ... I want you to be happy, Liza.

LAUREN. I am happy.

SETH. No, I want you to be happy. I'm pretty sure it is possible. Otherwise, how would we get through each day?

LAUREN. I'm happy.

SETH. But not really.

LAUREN. No. Not really.

SETH. Well, at least you're agreeing with me. *(He takes her in his arms.)*

## Scene 16

*Lauren is sitting at a table in the school cafeteria. Eliza walks by. She's sweaty and out of breath. She's wearing shorts and a tight shirt for the first time in the play.*

LAUREN. Liza — *(Eliza turns around.)*

ELIZA. What? *(Beat.)*

LAUREN. How are you? *(Eliza goes to Lauren's table.)*

ELIZA. Great, how are you?

LAUREN. Why are you all —

ELIZA. I joined the track team.

LAUREN. You did?

ELIZA. It's amazing. I never knew my body could do stuff like that. It's all about endurance, you know? And motivation. You really can get your body to do whatever you want it to if you try hard enough.

LAUREN. Oh.

ELIZA. And anyway, running's such a high. It's like, I don't know. Amazing.

LAUREN. I'm glad you're happy.

ELIZA. Oh I'm totally happy. *(Beat.)* How are you?

LAUREN. Fine.

ELIZA. Good. *(Beat.)* I guess we haven't talked in —

LAUREN. I know. A while.

ELIZA. Midterms suck, right?

LAUREN. Right. *(Beat.)* You look thin, Liza. *(Beat.)*

ELIZA. I know. I had no idea my thighs were so fat before.

LAUREN. They weren't —

ELIZA. You know, I just love shopping now. My mom and I have been going on these amazing sprees. You should see some of the stuff I've gotten. I mean, if you want to.

LAUREN. I want to.

ELIZA. Okay. Maybe one day you can come over and —

LAUREN. But I mean, Liza, aren't you eating anymore? People are saying —

ELIZA. It's none of your business.

LAUREN. I know.

ELIZA. Okay.

LAUREN. But why? You love to eat.

ELIZA. No, I don't.

LAUREN. Yes, you do. I mean … you kind of look like …

ELIZA. What?

LAUREN. Are you starving?

ELIZA. And just so you know. I'm not a lesbian. In case you care. I mean I've been thinking about it and I'm not.

LAUREN. Okay.

ELIZA. Anyway I better go. I've got study hall and you know how Jenkins gets if you're late.

LAUREN. Okay.

ELIZA. Okay.

LAUREN. Take care of yourself, Liza.

ELIZA. What are you, fifty?

LAUREN. No. *(Eliza walks away. She turns back as though to say something more but then thinks better of it and keeps going.)*

# Scene 17

*Lauren watches Seth sleep.*

SETH. What are you doing?
LAUREN. Don't wake up. You don't have to.
SETH. Okay. *(Beat.)*
LAUREN. Seth? Are you awake?
SETH. I guess so.
LAUREN. Can I tell you something?
SETH. Is everything all right?
LAUREN. I don't know.
SETH. *(Gently.)* What is it?
LAUREN. When we first met I wondered what you saw in me.
SETH. Well, you were hot.
LAUREN. I wondered why you'd want to be with someone like me. Because I know I'm not easy. And now I'm trying to figure out what's going on —
SETH. What's going on?
LAUREN. I mean, who we are. Like, sometimes I think you're someone else. And sometimes I'm someone else and it's getting really cloudy for me, really cloudy.
SETH. Who do you think you are?
LAUREN. This girl Eliza.
SETH. But you are —
LAUREN. I know it must feel like I'm hiding something from you.
SETH. Are you?
LAUREN. I think so.
SETH. You're a private person. You're just not used to this kind of thing yet.
LAUREN. No, I mean, yes, but ...
SETH. What are you hiding?
LAUREN. Here's a story. You might think it's stupid —
SETH. I won't.
LAUREN. But when I was kid, my best friend and I used to watch

this one movie over and over again. It wasn't even a good movie and we were like, I don't know, eleven, right? She'd come over and we'd just sit there and my mom didn't get it. She'd always ask if we wanted to watch something else but she let us do it, I think because it wasn't harmful and we enjoyed it.

SETH. Was it porn?

LAUREN. No, it wasn't porn. It doesn't even matter what it was. I mean, it was *Pretty Woman*. We saw it at my birthday party one year and got a real kick out of it, but that's not what kept us watching it.

SETH. Your mom let you watch *Pretty Woman* at eleven?

LAUREN. But the point of the story is ... it wasn't that every time the movie seemed like new, or that we kept finding fresh things in it. It was simply that this was what we did and it was comfortable and ... my friend and I ate sandwiches my mom made for us and drank juice and the afternoon just passed watching that movie. When it was over, it was dark and she went home and by then my mom had made dinner and we'd eat and the rest of the night would go as it always did.

SETH. It sounds nice.

LAUREN. Right. But *more* than nice. And that's what I can't get out of my mind. That ... I don't think we've found that movie yet.

SETH. What movie?

LAUREN. The one we could watch over and over.

SETH. You're not making sense. It's the middle of the night.

LAUREN. I am making sense, Seth.

SETH. Then what are you saying?

LAUREN. Don't get me wrong. I mean, I love you.

SETH. You do?

LAUREN. *(Dawning on her.)* Yes.

SETH. I know. I love you too.

LAUREN. But that's the problem. I mean, that's the problem.

SETH. Liza —

LAUREN. Do you know what I'm trying to tell you?

SETH. Um.

LAUREN. That I'm confused, or something? Or scared? That maybe I've gone too far down some road and I can't get off? That I can't get rid of the old movie? Are you hearing me? This is important, Seth. Please try.

SETH. Okay ... Yes, I think I've heard you. You need reassurance.

LAUREN. I do?

SETH.  I can give you that. We're going to watch so many movies.
LAUREN.  We are?
SETH.  And we'll talk about them. And sometimes we'll agree that one was really really good, like life-changingly good, and we'll buy it and memorize all the lines and watch it whenever we can.
LAUREN.  We will?
SETH.  Metaphorically.
LAUREN.  Is that what this is?
SETH.  Isn't it?
LAUREN.  I guess so … But —
SETH.  But what?
LAUREN.  I don't know … I'm sorry for waking you up.
SETH.  It's fine. You know that. *(He kisses her on the cheek and goes back to sleep. She continues to watch him.)*


## Scene 18


*Eliza is in the hospital. She's knitting and barely looks up. Lauren sits beside her.*


LAUREN.  So, how are you doing? *(Beat.)* This is a nice room. *(Beat.)* What are you making?
ELIZA.  Scarf.
LAUREN.  Cool.
ELIZA.  I mean, while I'm in this fucking place, I may as well get something done.
LAUREN.  It's not so bad, is it?
ELIZA.  Look around.
LAUREN.  Well, some of the people in here do look really … well, not good.
ELIZA.  I know. I'm like, why the fuck am I here?
LAUREN.  Well, it's a nice scarf.
ELIZA.  Yeah.
LAUREN.  I didn't know you could knit.
ELIZA.  And they won't let me exercise. Fuckers.
LAUREN.  But … don't you think you should be resting?

ELIZA.  And they want me to say things.

LAUREN.  Like what?

ELIZA.  They want me to say all these things that are such bull-shit. Like I'm angry because my dad died. Or because my mom was too needy. I tell them they're assholes ... But you know they say I might never get my period. And the problem is —

LAUREN.  What?

ELIZA.  I don't know.

LAUREN.  Liza —

ELIZA.  What? *(Beat.)*

LAUREN.  I mean, at least you have your own room, right?

ELIZA.  Whatever.

LAUREN.  You want to hear about school at all, or? *(Beat.)* Like, yesterday Mr. Halverson told us that if we wanted to write a long paper at the end of the semester we could skip all the reading quizzes and I thought that was a good idea and was sure we would decide to do that but then Julie Miller was like, "Well, how much will the paper be worth?" and he was like, "I haven't decided yet but a fair bit of your grade" and she was like "It's not worth it, guys" and then everyone was nodding and now we have to keep taking these ridiculous reading quizzes. *(Beat.)* Yeah, and then after class she — I mean, Julie — came up to me and was like, I heard you and Jason slept together, loud enough that other people could hear — and I was like, "Who are you to confront me in the hall-way about something like that?" *(Beat.)*

ELIZA.  You slept with Jason?

LAUREN.  Yeah. *(Beat.)*

ELIZA.  Congratulations.

LAUREN.  I wanted to tell you first.

ELIZA.  Thanks.

LAUREN.  Yeah. So. It was two nights ago. We were going to wait for the end of the school year but, well, Jason really wanted to and I figured what's the difference between now and June, right?

ELIZA.  *(Quietly.)* So how was it?

LAUREN.  Oh, amazing.

ELIZA.  Good.

LAUREN.  I mean, well, we were in his brother's room ... and the walls in there are brown and it's dark and it smells kind of like gym socks and some weird cologne. And then ... afterwards there were no candles and Jason didn't say much ...

ELIZA. Uh-huh —

LAUREN. No, I mean, it was great. It's just that, I mean, I figured … it would feel more different than this, not being something anymore. But really I'm just still … whatever I was.

ELIZA. So Julie found out about it?

LAUREN. Yeah, and I told her it was none of her business. And she said she heard it from a "confirmed" source and when I started walking away she said "Jason, Jason told me" and I turned around and slapped her. I don't know what came over me. (Beat. She waits for Eliza to speak, but she doesn't.) Anyway she looked so shocked. SO shocked. Like she'd just fallen down ten flights of stairs but had survived … But then she told me she'd slept with Jason too, before me. She told me they still hung out sometimes, which I think was supposed to mean that she still sleeps with him. She said she convinced him to go out with me because I needed some male attention. She said a lot of things … so I spat on her shoes. Her new shoes … and she kicked me. See? (Lauren lifts her leg to show Eliza a bruise.)

ELIZA. (Seriously.) That's because Julie is a total bitch. REAL

LAUREN. She's not a total bitch.

ELIZA. She kicked you and slept with your boyfriend.

LAUREN. I know.

ELIZA. You still like her?

LAUREN. I don't know. I guess so.

ELIZA. And Jason?

LAUREN. I'm, well, I'm meeting him later. To talk. Like maybe he'll tell me Julie was lying and —

ELIZA. Great friends.

LAUREN. Well you could be a little more sympathetic. I mean, I got suspended. And now my parents say I'm "acting out" and they think it's because of you. (Beat.)

ELIZA. Will you just go away, Lauren. I don't know why you keep coming here. (Beat.)

LAUREN. Because I'm worried about you.

ELIZA. Well, worry about yourself.

## Scene 19

*Seth and Lauren eat by candlelight.*

SETH. And I told Trev that if I went any longer without eating a burger — just a goddamned burger — I might go mad.

LAUREN. So you gave in?

SETH. I didn't give in. I surrendered. I gave myself wholeheartedly. It was the best burger I ever ate.

LAUREN. So you were a vegetarian for?

SETH. Three days freshman year. The worst three days.

LAUREN. And you didn't score a single chick?

SETH. Not a one.

LAUREN. Poor Seth.

SETH. College is tough for the heterosexual male. So much temptation everywhere. So much that's unattainable. It's cruel, really. The bank is much better. At least I'm not tempted all the time.

LAUREN. Hey!

SETH. Not that I want to be.

LAUREN. Do I still tempt you?

SETH. Yes.

LAUREN. How much?

SETH. Enough.

LAUREN. That's it.

SETH. More than enough.

LAUREN. Be careful what you say.

SETH. Why?

LAUREN. Once you say things you can't take them back.

SETH. I know. *(He leans over and kisses her. He stands. He goes off-stage.)*

LAUREN. What are you doing?

SETH. You'll see.

LAUREN. Seriously, what —

SETH. Hold your horses, honey.

LAUREN. You don't call me honey.

SETH. I just did. *(Seth returns with his guitar and begins to strum.)*

LAUREN. What's that?

SETH. Guitar.

LAUREN. Right, I meant — *(He begins to sing.)*
ELIZA ELIZA I OWE YOU A SONG
IT WON'T BE MUCH; IT WON'T TAKE LONG
BUT AS THAT BARD WAS KNOWN TO SIGH
"OUR REMEDIES OFT IN OURSELVES DO LIE"
AND ELIZA ELIZA I OWE YOU A SONG
DON'T JUDGE MY LYRICS; THEY'RE ALL WRONG
BUT OUT OF EVERYTHING I KNOW IN MY LIFE
ONE THING'S FOR SURE …

*(He stops playing.)* Will you be my wife? *(He takes a box from his jacket and opens it.)* I don't have a speech or anything. It's just that, I think this is the right thing. I know we haven't known each other for like ten years the way my parents did before they got married, but I don't think that matters. I love you, and the strange thing is, I have this feeling that my dad would have loved you too, which is something I haven't told you because I didn't want to freak you out, but now I'm freaking you out anyway, so I figured you should know. *(Beat.)* Well?

LAUREN. You've asked the wrong person.

SETH. What do you mean?

LAUREN. I mean … That's not my name.

SETH. What's not your name?

LAUREN. Eliza. That's not my name.

SETH. What are you talking about?

LAUREN. That. That's all. That's what I'm talking about. You've got the wrong girl. *(Lauren has stood and put on her jacket.)*

SETH. Where are you going?

LAUREN. I just have to get out of here.

SETH. Oh no. You're not leaving. Not again.

LAUREN. I am Seth. I am. I wanted to … do this, or something, or whatever this is but now I'm getting out of here. I can't … I can't do this anymore. I mean, I promised myself. I told myself. No one else. I told myself over and over. All that time. All these years. I told myself.

SETH. What are you talking about? You're not making any sense. *(Seth blocks her.)*

LAUREN. Seth. Get out of my way.

SETH. No.

LAUREN. The fact is, you don't love *me*. You don't even know me.
SETH. What do you mean? Of course I do.
LAUREN. No you don't. *(Beat.)* Let me go, Seth. *(She pushes past him and leaves.)*
SETH. Where are you going? I just proposed to you. Where are you going?

## Scene 20

*Eliza and Lauren. Eliza is still in the hospital. She's hooked up to a heart rate monitor.*

LAUREN. I bought you these, see? *(Eliza barely moves.)* Here, they're fun. *(Lauren slips a few bangle bracelets on Eliza's arm. They hang there.)* If you move your arm, they'll sparkle. *(Eliza doesn't move.)* But they're nice like that too, still. *(Beat.)* I mean, they weren't expensive. I got them at the pharmacy. I got myself some too — in pink. You wanna see?
ELIZA. Go away. Please. I don't want you to see me this way. *(Beat.)*
LAUREN. So what should we do?
ELIZA. I'm not happy.
LAUREN. I know.
ELIZA. I just want things to be the way they were.
LAUREN. I know.
ELIZA. I never have nice dreams anymore.
LAUREN. I know.
ELIZA. You do?
LAUREN. Yeah.
ELIZA. I'm not sure it's something you can understand unless you've been through it.
LAUREN. Oh. Well, that's probably true. *(Beat.)* So, do you want to play Monopoly? *(Eliza shakes her head.)* No. Do you want to watch a movie? I rented a few, just in case ... I even brought *Pretty Woman* ... *(Eliza shakes her head.)* Are you tired? *(Eliza nods.)* Okay. *(Eliza sleeps.)* Liza? ... Can you hear me? *(Beat.)* Because I wanted

to tell you I've been having this dream that it's like a year ago and we're just sitting on the floor of your room playing checkers and you beat me, over and over again, and then I wake up and I'm really happy. *(Beat.)* Liza … please don't give up. I mean, if you give up now, I'll never forgive you. Never. *(Beat.)* It'll break my heart.

## ❧ Scene 21

*Lauren is all alone in the large empty yoga room. She is sitting in the middle of the floor, not moving. After a long while a woman, played by the same actress as Eliza, enters.*

MEGAN. Oh! I'm sorry. I'm interrupting — *(Beat.)* Are you okay? *(Beat. Lauren doesn't even look up.)* If you want, I can leave. There might be another open room. If you want privacy.
LAUREN. *(Quietly, meaning "please leave.")* It's fine.
MEGAN. *(Not getting it at all.)* Okay! *(Megan spreads out her mat.)* I guess you're having a rough day too. I know I shouldn't say it; we've barely just met, but you'd think by my age, I'd have found a way to get over PMS, huh? But no. I'm as pissed off as ever. *(Beat.)* Now you definitely want me to leave, right? What an introduction. Megan.
LAUREN. What?
MEGAN. My name. Megan. And you? Do you have one?
LAUREN. Eliza.
MEGAN. No, you don't look like an Eliza. It's funny. I guess I knew one once.
LAUREN. *(More to herself.)* I did too.
MEGAN. I just started yoga. I find it incredibly calming. My therapist says I talk so much that I need to find something I can do in silence. So what do I do? I find you! There were other empty rooms. Don't tell.
LAUREN. Okay.
MEGAN. It just seemed so much nicer than going to the gym. I hate those machines, the way you strap in and stay there for forty-five minutes. It's like your brain's on hold while your body sweats. It's unnatural.

LAUREN. *(After a breath.)* I can't stand gyms.

MEGAN. This is the closest I could come. I like to take walks, really. But my doctor doesn't think it's cardiovascular enough. *(Beat.)* Let me know if you want me to be quiet. I can do that. I am capable. *(Long beat.)* I mean, it's been such a day already. What a breath of fresh air, huh? Just chatting. I swear, if I have to look another woman in the eye and ask her whether she's menstruating. God help me. *(Beat. Lauren stares at her.)* No — I'm a nurse. A nurse. *(Beat.)* What a world, eh?

LAUREN. Yeah.

MEGAN. How about you? What do you do?

LAUREN. I work with aquatic animals.

MEGAN. You're a marine biologist?

LAUREN. That's right.

MEGAN. You like the water?

LAUREN. Yeah, I guess so.

MEGAN. I hate it. Refused to learn to swim when I was a girl. All I would do was stand on the first step of the pool or in the shallowest part of the ocean and stare out at the deep. It seemed so daunting. And to this day, I won't put my whole head in. I like being able to breathe. Without breath, how do you feel alive, right?

LAUREN. In school, senior year of high school, I won the contest for staying longest underwater.

MEGAN. How long?

LAUREN. Oh, I think I nearly died. However long is almost too long.

MEGAN. Good lord. You and I are not the same.

LAUREN. You know, a man proposed to me the other day. *(Beat.)* I don't know why I'm telling you, but —

MEGAN. No, I love this stuff. Eat it up. What'd you say?

LAUREN. Well, I took off.

MEGAN. Oh honey. You don't love him?

LAUREN. I don't know.

MEGAN. I was once in a relationship with a man, let's call him Gus. He used to take me places, to parks, to sit in the empty pews of churches at midnight, to late-night movies, to small towns upstate. He was so good to me. Romantic, you know, and like I said I'm not very … romantic, just a late-bloomer I guess, and after awhile I got wary of all the nice things he did. They started seeming more … I don't know, manipulative than they really were. I stopped sleeping with him. Soon, we didn't even kiss. He moved to Vermont, I think, or maybe Maine? And I heard recently that he got married. You know how it goes.

LAUREN. Were you sad?

MEGAN. Yes. *(Beat.)* But did I have a right to be? There I'm not so sure.

LAUREN. I think you had a right to be.

MEGAN. Yeah? Well ... Life's so hard. One can't always blame oneself. We make so many decisions, some are bound to be wrong.

LAUREN. You know ... you remind me of someone. It's incredible, really.

MEGAN. Is that right?

LAUREN. Like a friend I once had —

MEGAN. All my life people have told me that. That I seem like someone else.

LAUREN. I miss her.

MEGAN. Who?

LAUREN. Eliza.

MEGAN. You have the same name? Cute.

LAUREN. No — I mean, yes. The same name. Had.

MEGAN. Was she nice?

LAUREN. Of course. I mean, she was very nice.

MEGAN. No one's very nice. Some people pass themselves off as nice tolerably well but we're animals, all of us.

LAUREN. No, she was ... she didn't have a cruel bone in her body.

MEGAN. She did. She hated people. She probably hated you for a while.

LAUREN. But I deserved it.

MEGAN. She thought you were mean.

LAUREN. And I am.

MEGAN. You were in school. You were a child ... You know, I went into a lot of people's private yoga rooms and no one else said a word to me.

LAUREN. What are you talking about? What do you mean I was a child —

MEGAN. I sensed, even then, that ...

LAUREN. That what?

MEGAN. You were a good person. I deal with so many people in the course of a day — people in less pain than you and they're unashamed about being malicious.

LAUREN. No. I promise you. I guarantee you. I'm not at all good —

MEGAN. You've been through the mill.

LAUREN. Who are you?

MEGAN. Who are you?

LAUREN. I'm …

MEGAN. You're wonderful.

LAUREN. That's what Seth says. I don't know what he sees in me.

MEGAN. He's lonely. He's reached the end of being alone. And he has nice hair — the way it sticks up a little, like an alien.

LAUREN. Eliza?

MEGAN. *(Standing to leave.)* Megan. I'm sorry — maybe I should go.

LAUREN. No!

MEGAN. You know, in my experience, life is what you make of it. If you decide you like gray days, then you like gray days. They're transformed.

LAUREN. But —

MEGAN. Right after my father died, when I was eleven, I told my mother that I wished she was dead too. We had a fight about R-rated movies; she didn't want me to go to a party where they would be watching *Pretty Woman* even though it was my best friend's party, and I said that awful thing and then she cried in a way she'd never cried before, not even after my father died.

LAUREN. You were upset.

MEGAN. But I said it. And at the time, I meant it.

LAUREN. Did you apologize?

MEGAN. Never. But my mother knew it wasn't how I really felt. She forgave me.

LAUREN. Oh God. Eliza?

MEGAN. No, there is no God.

LAUREN. This is a dream.

MEGAN. Then wake up.

LAUREN. What if I can't?

MEGAN. You can.

# Scene 22

*Lauren stands at Seth's front door, knocking. The whole scene has a fast and frantic quality. Even when she has Seth's attention, Lauren seems to be trying urgently to get it, to say something.*

LAUREN.  Um, Seth. Seth. It's … me. *(Beat.)* I know you're home because … well, I saw you walk home. You had a bag from Changs and I can smell your food, Peking Duck or something, so I know you're in there … and I feel like … I mean, I really need to see you. I mean, Seth, I really need to see you … I need to — *(Seth opens the door. Beat.)* You opened the door. *(Beat.)* So, hi. *(Beat.)* How are you?
SETH.  I'm not going to talk to you.
LAUREN.  But you opened the door. *(He begins to close the door.)* No! Seth. *(He opens the door a little.)*
SETH.  I'm not going to talk to —
LAUREN.  I have to tell you something! I have to; I have to.
SETH.  *(Opening the door, and angrily:)* Like what, that you're insane?
LAUREN.  No, Seth. I mean, yes, I mean in a way. Yes —
SETH.  Try making some sense. A coherent thought would be nice.
LAUREN.  Don't get mad, please —
SETH.  Don't get mad? Look, if you're crazy just tell me right now that you're crazy — because I mean, I thought … even though you were a little … mysterious … I thought I knew you. And it's not like I don't have my own problems, I mean — do I need this? Do I need someone so … messed up? How messed up are you exactly?
LAUREN.  Eliza died.
SETH.  Great.
LAUREN.  No, I mean. She was my best friend. And she died. When we were fourteen.
SETH.  Yup.
LAUREN.  I'm not lying.
SETH.  No, of course not.
LAUREN.  Please, Seth.
SETH.  Please, what?

LAUREN. I was just a kid.

SETH. Uh-huh.

LAUREN. And I made an awful mistake and ever since then, I've been, well, inside of it. It just goes on and on. Like I'm outside of time and I can't get back in.

SETH. You're outside of time.

LAUREN. *(Looking down, and quietly.)* And the problem is, there aren't punishments!

SETH. What are you talking about?

LAUREN. For little girls who do bad things. Who are mean and selfish and trying to grow up. There are no punishments. No one blamed me even though it was my fault, Eliza dying. I just went back to school and sat at my desk and ate my lunch and did my algebra homework. I just, I mean, did my homework like anyone else.

SETH. What do you mean it was your fault?

LAUREN. I abandoned her.

SETH. Like in a sinking ship, on a desert island? What are you trying to tell me?

LAUREN. I made other friends and I left her behind.

SETH. Uh-huh.

LAUREN. It was when she needed me most.

SETH. And?

LAUREN. And then she got very thin and sort of faded away. *(Beat.)*

SETH. And you think that was your fault?

LAUREN. I know it was.

SETH. When I was fourteen, my best friend was Mark Hickman. When I was fourteen and two weeks, Mark Hickman wouldn't look me in the eye, literally ran away from me down crowded hallways. I didn't kill myself.

LAUREN. No, for so long after she died, I didn't get out of bed. My parents thought I might never recover and they were right, in a way, even though I did eventually get out of bed and sort of go through the motions. That is, until I met you, when I thought, and I know this is crazy, I thought for the first time, wow, Eliza would have really liked this guy; she would have really liked him, the way he's unpretentious and open and caring and brave. That's the kind of man she would have liked. And so ... I don't know ... I just said her name. Because she was with me anyway. Because it just came out that way —

SETH. God.

LAUREN. And I was okay for a while because everything was new, because it hadn't gotten serious.

SETH. Uh-huh.

LAUREN. But then things got confusing because I still couldn't give her up, even when I wanted to —

SETH. Liza —

LAUREN. Seth, my name's Lauren. *(Beat.)*

SETH. Lauren.

LAUREN. Lauren. *(Beat.)* And I can show you where I grew up and I can meet your friends and you can meet my parents, even though they'd be shocked that you really exist, that anyone exists who could have helped me ... emerge. And you can call me at work even though I kind of keep to myself there and people would talk if I got a call. I mostly spend my time underwater, in the tanks, running tests. But now I don't want to. I don't want to anymore. I don't want to anymore.

SETH. Lauren.

LAUREN. I don't know. Maybe we can at least be friends? If ...

SETH. I don't want to be your friend.

LAUREN. Okay.

SETH. It's just that ... and this is me talking and not my therapist or Trevor or anyone. It's just that, I can't keep putting myself through, well, this, or you, I mean. I can't keep putting myself through you.

LAUREN. I know.

SETH. If I could, I would.

LAUREN. I understand that.

SETH. I'm sorry.

LAUREN. I'm sorry too. *(Long beat.)*

SETH. But what do you think.

LAUREN. What do you mean?

SETH. It's possible.

LAUREN. What is?

SETH. Happiness.

LAUREN. Oh. I don't know.

SETH. But take a stab at it. *(Beat.)*

LAUREN. Okay, I think it's possible.

SETH. You do?

LAUREN. Yes.

SETH. Why?

LAUREN. Well otherwise, how would we get through each day?

## Scene 23

*A flashback. Lauren and Eliza are lying on a bed, side by side; they're eleven.*

LAUREN. So, Julie Miller and I are going to go on a walk later today. She says some of the farms near her dad's house are haunted. Do you want to come?

ELIZA. I don't think this is the right time for me to be touring haunted houses.

LAUREN. Oh, right, sorry … But, well, I think there are some fields too. And cows. Maybe you should get some fresh air. It might be good for you. Don't people say that? Plus I don't want to be alone with Julie Miller. She talks so much.

ELIZA. Not today. *(Beat.)*

LAUREN. Don't you want to talk about it, Liza?

ELIZA. No.

LAUREN. If I were you, I'd want to talk about it. I'd have to. I couldn't keep all that bottled up.

ELIZA. Well, we're not the same.

LAUREN. I'd never seen someone … dead before.

ELIZA. Neither had I.

LAUREN. Do you believe in heaven?

ELIZA. I don't know.

LAUREN. Did your dad?

ELIZA. I don't know. *(Beat.)*

LAUREN. I'm sorry — I shouldn't have asked that.

ELIZA. No, I just wish I knew.

LAUREN. Maybe your mom knows.

ELIZA. It's not the same.

LAUREN. No. *(Beat.)* But the funeral was really nice. What your mom said. And your grandpa.

ELIZA. Yeah.

LAUREN. I mean, it was really nice. I wish someone would say such nice things about me when I die.

ELIZA. Lauren.

LAUREN. Yeah?

ELIZA. What do you think happens when we die?

LAUREN. I don't know.

ELIZA. But what do you think?

LAUREN. My mom says —

ELIZA. No, what do *you* think?

LAUREN. I don't know ... I think ... it's probably very quiet.

ELIZA. Yeah, I agree.

LAUREN. And probably very warm, just the right temperature.

ELIZA. Yeah, that sounds right.

LAUREN. And probably you have the wildest dreams.

ELIZA. Wow, yeah.

LAUREN. So that you're not alone. *(Eliza curls up closer to Lauren; she puts her head on her chest.)*

ELIZA. I don't want my dad to be alone.

LAUREN. No, he's having wonderful dreams.

ELIZA. Do you think he's dreaming about me?

LAUREN. Oh, definitely.

ELIZA. He never got to see me graduate high school or get married or have a baby.

LAUREN. He's going to dream all those things.

ELIZA. But it's so sad.

LAUREN. It is.

ELIZA. And my mother's so sad.

LAUREN. I know. My mother said she didn't know what she'd do ... if it happened to her. *(Eliza takes Lauren's hand and curls closer.)* I don't know what she would do. She's so reliant on my father. He's like ... what wakes her up. Literally, I mean. Alarm clocks don't work for her anymore.

ELIZA. I'm so sad, Lauren. What if I'm sad forever?

LAUREN. *(Stroking Eliza's hair.)* You won't be.

ELIZA. How do you know?

LAUREN. I just do. You're very resilient.

ELIZA. What does that mean?

LAUREN. I don't know. I think I read it somewhere. But it seemed to apply to you.

ELIZA. Well, thank you.

LAUREN. Of course.

ELIZA. I'll always have you, right, Lauren?

LAUREN. Of course.

ELIZA. You promise?

LAUREN. I promise. *(They stare at each other; Lauren keeps stroking Eliza's hair. She pauses and then leans in and kisses Eliza, on the lips.)*

ELIZA. *(Quietly.)* What are you doing?

LAUREN. I don't know. *(She kisses her again. It's very tender.)* You're my best friend, Liza.

ELIZA. I know. You're my best friend too.

## End of Play

# PROPERTY LIST

Yoga mats
Flyer for "Inner Voice" class
Pillows (change cases to use same pillows for scenes)
Fashion magazine (circa 1990s)
Box of cassette tapes
Tape player
Bangle bracelets
Wine glass
Check folder (and other restaurant paraphernalia, if desired)
Tea cup and saucer
Picnic basket w/grapes, wine, crackers, cheese
Folded sheet (to use as picnic blanket)
Cordless phone (circa 1990s)
"Caboodle" makeup case with lipstick, mascara, blush and brush
Hairbrush
Newspaper
Box of cereal
Guitar
Modern cordless phone
Bag of carrots
Pink prom dress (circa 1990s)
Tray w/small milk carton, plate of food, fork, knife
Knitting needles with half-finished scarf
Ring box with engagement ring
Hospital pillows
Hospital blanket
Rolling IV stand